Borderline Personality Disorder

A Complete BPD Guide for Improving Your Social Skills, Managing Your Emotions, Stop Anxiety, Overcoming Depression, Rewire Your Brain, and Improve Your Relationships

Perry Potter

Table of Contents

INTRODUCTION

Borderline personality disorder is a mental health condition that affects how you think and behave to yourself and others, making it difficult to function normally in daily life. Self-esteem issues, trouble controlling emotions and actions, and a history of dysfunctional relationships are all part of it.

With borderline personality disorder, you have a deep fear of abandonment or instability, and you may have difficulty tolerating being alone. However, outrageous anger, impulsiveness, and frequent mood swings can drive others away, even though you want to have long-lasting, loving relationships.

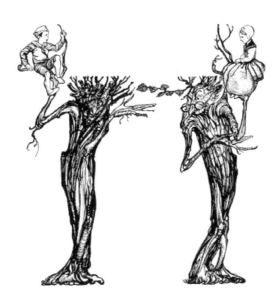

The onset of borderline personality disorder is normally in early adulthood. Early adulthood tends to be the worst time for the disorder, but it may improve with age.

Don't give up if you have borderline personality disorder. Many people with this condition will learn to live a full life with the help of therapy.

BORDERLINE

Borderline personality disorder (Borderline) has its origins in psychoanalytic understanding of those affected as a transitional area of neurotic and psychotic disorders, as symptoms from each have been identified according to the World Health Organization's (WHO) classification system.

Borderline personality disorder is now considered to be a subset of emotionally unstable people (comorbidity). In recent years, our understanding of the clinical picture has greatly expanded. As a result, it is assumed that the development of borderline disorder is caused by a combination of genetic factors and, in many cases, early traumatic experiences. More than half of those affected report severe abuses, over 60% emotional neglect, and almost all of them describe a social atmosphere in which they felt alien, vulnerable, and embarrassed.

Around 3% of the population suffers from a borderline illness. Adolescence is normally when the first symptoms appear. Even though slightly more women seek treatment, it appears that about the same number of men as women are affected. More than 60% of those affected have attempted suicide at least once, demonstrating the value of treatment.

The word "borderline" has a complicated past. It was first used to characterize a disorder that straddled the line between neurosis and psychosis. The "relationship" between borderline personality disorder and schizophrenia is no longer assumed in today's definition.

The result of the examination shows that Borderline personality disorder is a distinct mental illness with a wide range of symptoms. The word's original definition is no longer true. Many that have been affected, on the other hand, are very familiar with the sense of the word: on the edge of normalcy and sickness, closeness and distance. Many border crossers have been injured at the border and find it difficult to set boundaries.

Borderline personality disorder is an unusual and sometimes misunderstood condition. People with borderline disorders struggle most with their relationships and in their self-esteem. They have trouble controlling their emotions and mood, and they always behave rashly. Scratches and suicide attempts are common forms of self-injury. The more one learns about the illness, the more one understands the pain and isolation of those who are affected. That is why it is critical to discuss this problem.

Emotional and affective dysfunction, rage outbursts, anxiety attacks, and weakness in one's view of oneself and others. These are the main characteristics of borderline personality disorder (BPD), which shares some characteristics with mood disorders, particularly bipolar disorder. There is an alternation between euphoria and sadness in all clinical cases. Mood swings and emotional dysfunction in borderline disorder are context-dependent, i.e. they occur more often in interpersonal relationships.

Image by Edvard Munch

BORDERLINE SYNDROME
CAUSES

Borderline personality disorder is a type of personality disorder. Even the term "personality disorder" means that a stable personality exists. Many factors influence a person's personality, or what defines them.

The birth of a child is the beginning of the growth of a person's personality. Meanwhile, it is assumed that personality development begins in the womb.

Personality evolves as a result of genetic factors as well as life experiences. It's also crucial to consider how events are processed. Only mediated perceptions become a part of and form one's own personality. As a result of the interaction of perceptions, temperament, and mental processing of the learned, the personality emerges.

A personality disorder may occur if the development of one's personality is severely disrupted. This means that traumatic experiences combined with unfavorable predispositions will result in a negative personality growth. In the case of Borderline, the patient is both affected by his surroundings and by himself. The ramifications are well-known.

Of course, it's fascinating to learn how each patient's personality disorder developed and what caused it.But, to disillusion, one must admit that science is still in the dark about what these causes are, and what causes which disease manifestations. As a result, there are no definite signs that signal the onset of a borderline illness. Many variables must come together to establish a borderline illness, according to experts.

One of these factors is a person's genetic disposition, which is unique to each individual. Environmental factors, such as experiences and traumas, as well as neurological or biochemical disorders, all play a role.

Three factors, according to researchers, must be present for a borderline condition to develop:

These factors are:

> An environmental factor: traumas in childhood
> Genetic factor: the temperament
> Interaction between the first two factors

To understand this is like this: If a person has had to experience one or more traumas, and if his temperament, pre-programmed by his genes, is such that he cannot process these traumas, he may become ill with a borderline disorder.

Factors in the Environment

Three types of environmental causes, or traumas, were identified.

Type I

Unhappy childhood memories

A parent's separation or divorce, parents who are unable to empathize with the child, and so on). This trauma is distressing, but it can be remedied by loving care of the child once more.

Type II

Verbal and Emotional Abuse

These can be either verbal or emotional in nature. This may involve constant neglect of the infant, constant ranting or shutting down, or even a restriction imposed by the parents' mental illness.

Type III

Physical abuse

This involves physical or sexual abuse of an infant. However, such a trauma can also be caused by the parents' mental disorder or drug problems. The family life is constantly disrupted. The children are not given any assistance; instead, they are subjected to criticism or disinterest.

Many Borderliners, in truth, have been through at least one of these traumas, if not more. According to several reports, Borderliners had a tough childhood. Many borderline patients have been subjected to maltreatment or neglect as children.

Fear of death, intense helplessness, extreme anxiety, and an inability to process the experience are examples of these traumas. Many patients were physically, emotionally, or sexually abused as children, according to research.

Up to 70% of people have been sexually abused, and up to 50% have been physically abused. Members of the family deceived 50 percent of those who were sexually abused, sometimes for months or years. This typically happened before the age of twelve for women. Emotional deprivation shaped the lives of about 80% of Borderliners during their childhood.

Five factors, among others, were explored in greater depth, as they often occur in connection with borderline:

- Separation or divorce - loss of a parent

- disturbed relationship with the parents

- Abuse

- Genetic predisposition to mental illness

- Early disorders

Separation or divorce - loss of a parent

Many borderline patients had been split from one parent during their first year of life, according to researchers. Around 60% of Borderliners have undergone parental separation or have lost one parent as children or toddlers. This cause is important to other people who are suffering from mental illnesses. The death of a parent or the separation or divorce of parents seems to be a significant pillar in the development of the borderline syndrome.

Relationship with Parents is Strained.

Many Borderlines said they had a tense relationship with one or both of their parents. They also complain about poor education. According to studies, borderline patients' childhoods are frequently marked by criticism, aggression, conflict, and disorder.

The mother-daughter relationship is always strained. Conflicts or a significant distance may trigger this.A poor relationship with the father is also bad: if the father shows very little dedication to the child's relationship, the first pillar can be set on the edge.Worst of all, there's a tense relationship between both parents.

While in families where only one parent has a strained relationship with the child, the other will make up for it, it is "natural" for the child to be ignored and overlooked in such situations.

What does it Mean to be Abused?

Abuse encompasses a wide range of behaviors that can be perpetrated by both men and women.

Sexual, physical, and emotional violence are the most common forms. Abuse is often directed at a weaker person: a physically stronger man on a woman (or, in rare instances, the other way around), an adult on a boy, or a leader on his subordinates. There are, however, several other constellations that we will not mention here.

Violence of the physical kind

This is a situation involving physical assault. It is slapped, punched, sliced, stung, and so on; it is bruised, kicked, and bitten, cut, and so on.

Forced sexuality in the broadest sense is referred to as sexual abuse.

Kisses, forced sexual intercourse, rape, penis abuse, compulsive participation in group sex, the insertion of objects, sexual torture, ritual sexual abuse, and so on are all examples of sexual abuse.

Abuse of the mind

The spirit has been abused.

Children are often abandoned, left alone, lied to, mocked and imprisoned, and so on. In a nutshell, something that causes the soul to suffer.

Indifference

You deprive someone of love, comfort, and concern, among other things.

All of these types of violence, including neglect, cause long-term psychological damage. If you are unable to function in treatment, the majority of this trauma will last a lifetime.

The cornerstone of the borderline syndrome is early childhood conditions. So-called early disorders, according to psychoanalysis, contribute to borderline illness. The four early disorders listed below are especially common in borderliners:

- Individuality that has been distorted
- Disorders of connection
- Feelings and opinions that have been suppressed
- Climate that is invalidating

Individuality that has been distorted

In the second and third years of life, everybody realizes that he is special. You become conscious of your own body and willpower.

The child knows that he or she is self-sufficient and autonomous from others, but that he or she is still dependent on others. The child discovers that it can defy others' demands. Children as young as two years old, for example, recognize themselves in photographs, speak about themselves, and enter the so-called defiance process.

Children of this age have a strong desire to learn more about themselves and get beyond the limits set by their parents.

However, in order for this transition to be effective, parents and other caregivers must be on board. Disturbances can occur if this support is not provided.

A healthy sense of self means:

• You learn to be alone

• One bears fear

• One bears guilt

• You can empathize with others

• One recognizes his interests

• The reality is better known

• You can stand more stress

You can handle external disturbances better

You cultivate a positive attitude about your own body.

Disorders in early childhood, in particular (and hence early disorder), pave the groundwork for a borderline illness.

Parents who do not help their children develop positive self-esteem, for example, by withholding affection, punishing them, or providing excessive reward and security, run the risk of their child developing a mental illness.

It is particularly critical that during this time in their lives, even the tiniest threats voiced or implied lead them to fear of being abandoned. And it is precisely this fear of abandonment that quickly suffocates self-esteem growth. Children have internal conflicts. On the one hand, they want to develop their personalities; on the other hand, they are concerned that by doing so, their parents' affection will be lost. Kids, on the other hand, suppress their personalities because they know they depend on at least one parent.

Experiences that are traumatic

The so-called splitting off can also lead to a borderline condition. When a child is exposed to abuse, conflict, disorder, power, the regular effects of separation, or excessive guarding, a defense mechanism known as "splitting off" is triggered. This suggests that the child ignores the negative aspects of his life because he knows that he can depend on his parents to help him survive. To be able to function emotionally in this world, the child fully ignores the negative aspects and instead sees the positive aspects of an otherwise dysfunctional family. It does, however, contain fear or rage, which a child alone cannot effectively manage.

However, this psychic trick of breaking off has a significant drawback: the creation of one's sense of self is disrupted. Since the bad is still concealed and all that remains is automatically positive, the child never learns to establish a proper weighing of good and bad.

Disorders of Connection

A so-called attachment disorder may also be a factor in the stifling of healthy self-esteem growth. Many Borderliners have had childhood experiences in which their family provided a safe haven while still posing a threat and causing anxiety.

This is most common when children receive insufficient care and attention, their feelings and needs are overlooked, or their parents are untrustworthy. The children lose confidence in their caregivers over time and do not learn how to coexist in a normal social setting. They move away from him, leaving no one nearby.

Feelings and opinions that have been suppressed.

Growing up in a stressful atmosphere makes it difficult for children to process negative experiences and their own feelings. They are made to believe that their environments are natural for them and that negative feelings towards them are suppressed. As a result, they develop an unsettling relationship with life over time, and they perceive the world as beneficial to them despite the negative aspects.

Furthermore, these children never learn to properly classify their own feelings, whether right or wrong, bad or good, and they suppress those thoughts to the greatest extent possible. They also make an effort to avoid considering their own wants, emotions, or needs.

Unfortunately, this means that these children will never know how another person feels or thinks. They are unable to distinguish others' intentions, or they misspoke a spoken phrase.

Invalidating the surroundings

When a child is given so little compassion or empathy, it creates an invalidating atmosphere. Violence, contempt, or slander of the child can occur in extreme cases.

Children believe that their opinions and emotions are unimportant to others and that they are ignored. Often their expressions of their thoughts and emotions are mocked or punished.

By the way, invalid is an English word that means "invalid," because the kids understand that their ideas are invalid, or in this case, unacceptable or incorrect. The child believes that his/her emotions and ideas are not permitted.

As a result, the infant never learns to become conscious of their own thoughts and feelings, nor does he or she learn to properly describe their thoughts and feelings.

Furthermore, children do not learn to trust their own feelings or to be able to depend on them.

Children in such an atmosphere, on the other hand, discover that they are only taken seriously if they exhibit extreme reactions. Unfortunately, these intense reactions are often well beyond what is considered natural in healthy individuals.

NEGATIVE CONSEQUENCES AMASSING

Many "small" causes that by themselves may not be enough to cause a borderline condition can add up to severe trauma in the end. In addition, most children lack family and social systems, which aids in the development of a personality disorder. Since these negative factors normally impact a child for a prolonged period of time, the child's ability to process them ultimately deteriorates.

IS POST-TRAUMATIC STRESS DISORDER (PTSD) A BORDERLINE DISORDER?

One might infer from this that such trauma is the root cause of borderline disease. Is borderline syndrome a form of post-traumatic stress disorder that lasts a long time?

This implies that the signs are almost identical. Borderliners share symptoms with people suffering from post-traumatic stress disorder in up to 50% of cases. This means they have the same symptoms as people who have just been through a traumatic event.

However, it contradicts the fact that extreme childhood trauma can cause a variety of diseases, not just borderline syndrome. Furthermore, not everybody who was neglected or mistreated as a child becomes a Borderliner.

As a result, the Borderline diagnosis should not be confused with chronic post-traumatic stress disorder.

What is Post-Traumatic Stress Disorder (PTSD) and how does it affect you?

Post-traumatic stress disorder affects about 25% of people who have been exposed to extreme trauma, such as sexual or physical abuse, disasters, conflict, or even torture.

The following are the most common signs and symptoms of this condition.

- Panic and fear
- inner turmoil
- sleep disturbances
- a lack of perseverance
- jitteriness

Flashbacks occur in those that are affected, and the event recurs in dreams or mental images.

Many that have been impacted avoid going to locations, seeing people, or being in situations that remind them of the trauma.

Posttraumatic stress disorder may develop right after a traumatic event or weeks or months later. So, you always believe that the person in question has processed the traumatic situation, but you don't know until it's too late that it has really left deep wounds in the soul.

SYNDROME OF THE BORDERLINE

So, what exactly is Borderline Personality Disorder?

There are nine distinct characteristics to look for:

The survivor does not want to be alone, wishes to escape separations, and most importantly, does not want to be alone. Interpersonal relationships are intense, but often volatile, with hate and love often alternating. The person in question has a strange identity. His self-perception is skewed. The person in question is extremely impulsive. He still lives in denial of his defeats. Suicide and self-injury are often threatened by the survivor.

The person in question is noticeably unbalanced and erratic. Anxiety, irritability, and depressed moods are often observed. These moods, however, are only available for a limited time.

The person is dissatisfied and bored.

The individual who is afflicted is unable to control his anger.

In stages, the person in question misunderstood everyone; in times of crisis, he went totally silent. He feels alienated and transformed.

The victim does not want to be alone and wants to stop being separated, so

Borderliners can't stand being single. They are still afraid of being abandoned in any relationship, whether it is with their parents, friends, or spouse. This anxiety can be caused by even minor events, such as a phone call that is received late, a date that is canceled, or a disagreement over a trifle.

Also, a brief absence from the partner is often misinterpreted as a final abandonment.

A Borderliner soon joins new relationships so that they are not alone and are not left alone. They are, however, normally short-lived, as the new partner is initially idealized, but minorities later accuse them of negligence or non-observance. In addition, Borderliners make a lot of compromises in relationships that aren't ideal for either party in the long run.

The person in question has a strange identity. His self-perception is skewed.

Borderliners also have no idea who they are. They have no idea where they came from, what they look like, what their strengths and weaknesses are, what they can do, what they want, what experiences they have had, what is important and right for them, what is bad or good for them, or who they want to be with. They have no idea what ideals they should uphold, what they are not permitted to do, if they are sexually driven, or what motivates or relaxes them. They are unaware of themselves; they are unaware of their emotions, ideas, and feelings.

The person in question is extremely impulsive. He still lives in denial of his defeats.

Borderliners are impulsive and have a hard time managing themselves. Furthermore, the threshold for external or internal stimulation is much smaller in sick people than in healthy people. As a result, they respond to all perceptions and observations more strongly than others. Of course, this is particularly dangerous for people who are prone to self-harm. Harm to one's own body is one example, but risk-averse behavior, such as when driving a car or in social situations, such as contract negotiations, is another.

Borderliners are frequently vulnerable to rejection or separation, which may lead to suicide or self-harm. They express a desire to avoid being lost.

Threats of suicide or self-harm are used to alleviate pressure on those who are affected and to try to restore some kind of order. They often re-establish communication with reality for themselves as a result of this.

The person in question is noticeably unbalanced and erratic. Anxiety, irritability, and depressed moods are often observed. These moods, however, are only available for a limited time.

The fact that Borderlines respond strongly to external and internal stimuli has an impact on daily feelings and experiences such as love, rage, guilt, and grief, making her emotional life especially strong. This causes mood swings, and a Borderline is utterly helpless in the face of them.

Many borderline people experience a sense of inner emptiness and boredom, which can contribute to low self-esteem. This emptiness or boredom may strike unexpectedly, even though life had previously appeared to be complete. A Borderline soon develops the belief that only others can make life meaningful due to their inability to be alone, as well as feelings of emptiness and boredom.

The individual who is afflicted is unable to control his anger.

Many borderlines are annoyed, irritated, or frustrated all of the time. They frequently experience a lot of internal conflict. Their impulsivity and inability to manage it often lead to disputes with others, which can result in a heated argument or even a fist fight.

In stages, the person in question is misunderstood by everyone; in times of crisis, he went totally silent. He has weird and changed feelings about himself.

Stress causes those who are affected to lose their faith in the world as well as their faith in themselves. All seems to be evil; they feel tortured, and their sense of self has vanished. The sufferer feels like he or she is in a movie when the world loses its sense.

Other symptoms, in addition to the normal ones, can appear, such as:

• Depressive disorders

• Compulsive behavior

• Derealization / loss of reality

• Identity loss/depersonalization

• Phobias

• Hysteria

• Conventional black-and-white thinking

• Habits and compulsions

• Psychiatric signs and symptoms

• Attempts to Avoid Injuries

• Tingling sensations

• Erratic social behavior

• A problem with food

Diagnosis of Borderline Personality Disorder

The abbreviation ICD stands for "International Statistical Classification of Diseases and Related Health Problems". This classification was prepared by the World Health Organization (WHO) and is also mandatory for psychological and psychotherapeutic diagnostics.

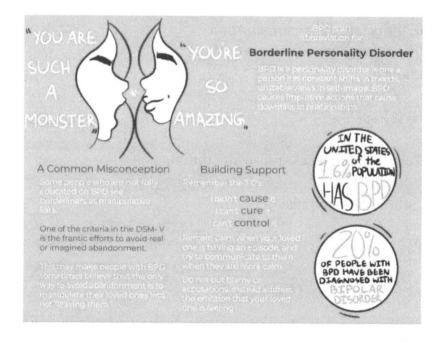

Emotionally unstable personality disorder

A personality disorder with a clear tendency to act impulsively without consideration of consequences, combined with an unpredictable and moody mood. There is a tendency for emotional outbursts and an inability to control impulsive behavior. There is also a tendency for contentious behavior and conflict with others, especially when impulsive acts are thwarted or obstructed. A distinction can be made between two manifestations: an impulsive type, predominantly characterized by emotional instability and lack of impulse control, and a borderline type, additionally characterized by disturbances of the self-image, the goals and the inner preferences, by a chronic feeling of emptiness.

There are two groups:

F60.30 Impulsive type

F60.31 Borderline type

F60.30 Impulsive type

The main character traits are emotional instability and lack of impulse control. Outbreaks of violent and threatening behavior are common, especially when criticized by others.

At least three of the following characteristics or behaviors must be present, including:

Clear tendency to act unexpectedly without taking into account the consequences, a clear tendency to quarrels and conflicts with others, especially when impulsive actions are suppressed or blamed.

The tendency of outbreaks of anger or violence with the inability to control explosive behaviors

Difficulties in retaining actions that are not directly rewarded, volatile and unpredictable moods.

F60.31 Borderline Type

There are some hallmarks of emotional instability, and in addition, one's self-image, goals, and "inner preferences" (including sexual ones) are often unclear and disturbed. Mostly there is a chronic feeling of inner emptiness. The tendency for intense but volatile relationships can lead to repeated emotional crises with excessive efforts not to be abandoned and suicidal or self-injurious acts. (These can also occur without significant triggers).

At least three of the criteria mentioned in F60.30 above must be present, plus at least two of the following characteristics and behaviors:

- Disorders and insecurity regarding self-image, goals and "inner preferences" (including sexual)
- The tendency to engage in intense but unstable relationships, often resulting in emotional crises
- Exaggerated efforts to avoid abandonment
- Repeats threats or acts with self-harm
- Persistent feelings of emptiness.

Diagnostic and Statistical Manual for Mental Disorders (DSM) of the American Psychiatric Association

DSM - IV

- A desperate effort to prevent a real or imaginary abandonment (except suicide or self-mutilation).

- An intense pattern of unstable, intense interpersonal relationships characterized by a shift between the two extremes of superannuation and devaluation.

- Identity disorder: Persistent and clearly disturbed, distorted or unstable self-image or feeling for one's own person (e.g. the feeling of not existing or embodying evil).

- Impulsiveness in at least two potentially self-destructive activities (spending, sexuality, substance abuse, shoplifting, reckless driving, bingeing - except suicide or self-mutilation).

- Repeated suicide threats, gestures or attempts or self-mutilating behaviors.

- Affective instability: marked mood swings (e.g., euphoria, irritability, anxiety), which usually last for a few hours, more rarely for more than a few days.

- A chronic feeling of emptiness.

- Excessive, strong anger or inability to control anger (e.g., frequent outbursts of anger, ongoing rage, or repeated beatings).

- Temporary, stress-related, severe dissociative symptoms or paranoid delusions

In addition, at least five of the following criteria must be met for a borderline disorder to be present (DSM-IV):

- Desperate effort to prevent real or imaginary being alone.

- A pattern of unstable and intense interpersonal relationships.

- Identity disorders: A pronounced instability of the self-image or the feeling for oneself.

- Impulsiveness in at least two potentially self-damaging areas (e.g., spending money, sex, substance abuse, reckless driving, gagging).

- Recurrent suicide threats, indications or attempts or self-injurious behavior.

- Affective instability characterized by a pronounced orientation to the current mood (e.g. severe episodic depression, irritability or anxiety).

- A chronic feeling of emptiness.

- Unreasonably strong anger or difficulty controlling anger or anger (e.g. frequent outbursts of anger, persistent anger, repeated beatings).

- Temporary stress-dependent paranoid ideas or severe dissociative symptoms.

Not all sufferers inflict injuries themselves and not all are addicted to addiction. However, borderline disorder usually occurs together with other diseases and disorders.

Depending on the composition of the criteria and the severity in the individual case, the further steps and the type of therapy are determined.

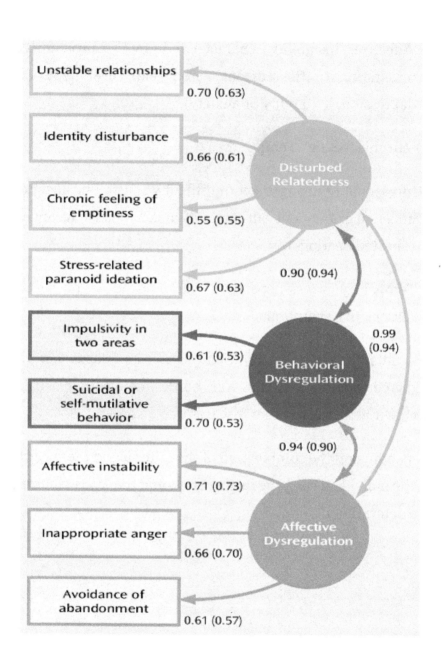

THE EMERGENCY BAG

When it's time again, when the pressure gets out of hand or when you feel empty inside: small things that bring you back to life and release the pressure. Because if you are in an unbearable situation, you should try to interrupt them immediately. But you do not have to hurt yourself, take drugs or buy pointless stuff, it's also different.

Here is a small emergency bag, which you always carry with you so that the help is quickly at hand:

For the body

Feeling and to relieve pressure: Sour or hot candy

Horse Mint Oil (a few drops on the back of the hand and lick it)

Chilli

A hard brush

Pebbles - Put in the shoe when needed

Chewing gums - The rather sharp variant

Knetball

Effervescent tablets - To take directly to the

Gum for the wrist

Cool pack (cold packs, which are cooled in the refrigerator and placed on the skin if necessary)

Extra hot mustard

For distraction:

MP3 player with relaxing music or your favorite music.

Telephone numbers of friends to talk to

Favorite stuffed toy

Perfume or fragrant oils

Chocolate - But please in moderation

Plasticine, kneading ball, sandbag to beat it on - to react and distract

Showers with the favorite shower gel

Creaming with matching milk or lotion

Souvenir photos

Postcards which onerejoiced over has

Loving letters that you got

Emails that have built up a mystery, or crosswords or similar

Videos or DVDs with beautiful children's films - for the injured child in us

Please note

Effervescent tablets, peppermint oil, chilli or similar should not get in the eye and used too often as there may be a health risk. Please do not put cold packs on the skin for too long. Otherwise, local frostbite can occur.

EMERGENCY LIST FOR
BORDERLINER

If you are hospitalized by an acute incident, the treating physicians should know which condition underlies your condition. Therefore, it is important to make an emergency list, which should contain all the important points that inform the doctors about your health status.

In addition to the name and address, etc., a list should include people whom you can contact if necessary.

In addition, the list should include the following items:

The psychiatric diagnosis, also with International Classification of Disease (ICD) key

A somatic diagnosis

The prescribed medication, in what dosage

Medicines that you should not or do not want

Name and address of the attending physician, do not forget phone number

It should also be noted that any existing old or new injuries could come from a borderline fault.

Do you have pets, or do you need to look after other people, such as children? Note this. Otherwise, they may stay alone for a long time, and nobody cares!

Do you have special skills that will help you especially well? If so, the clinicians may be able to help you get your supplies.

Such a list should always be carried with you because you never know what will happen.

You can also submit this list to your doctor, who can add more points if necessary. The emergency list should be completed more and more over time so that a complete picture of your condition arises.

Incidentally, such a list is also quite good if you do not come to a hospital emergency, such as a routine examination. Thus, the treating doctors in the hospital already know in advance what they have to pay attention to.

SELF-HELP SHEET FOR A BORDERLINER

The self-help form should allow borderline sufferers to keep their own self-help potential in mind. This makes it possible to make rapid use of it in crisis situations, even when the internal pressure is just too great, and you only have emptiness in your head.

So take some time and fill out this sheet carefully. Experience has shown that this list can be extended from time to time when you have discovered or learned something new.

In addition, as you work on this arc, your own understanding of your difficulties and relationships with specific situations will be enhanced.

And of course it should also be said that this list does not replace therapy.

If I notice during the filling out that I feel worse, who should I talk to?

_____

_____

_____

If   I   notice,   then   I   speak   about   it   with

_____

Strengthen your own mental defense.

Just as you can strengthen your physical defense, so you can also strengthen your mental defense. And that is very important for borderline patients.

So how can I consolidate my psyche? What is good for me? How do I avoid stress?

You've probably already noticed that in good times you can easily do something that will do you good. But in difficult times you will not succeed.

So what do you do, for example, when you are well, that you feel better?

_____

_____

_____

What could you do with it if you are not feeling well?

_____

_____

_____

What do you normally enjoy doing, and are you doing well?

_____

_____

_____

What do you think you need especially to be mentally well? (So, for example, adequate sleep, exercise, a fixed daily routine)

_____

_____

_____

What behavior brings me in a short time completely out of balance? Something you should avoid so necessarily!

_____

_____

_____

What causes my balance in the medium term? So you must not do this over a longer period! By contrast, what do you enjoy doing when you do it for a long time?

_____

_____

_____

_____

What could I do to maintain my balance? (E.g. more with friends or something similar)

_____

_____

_____

_____

Learning to recognize and avoid special burdens

Borderliners have great difficulty in dealing with demands. They are quickly overpowered by it. Sometimes you do not even realize what really bothers them so much. So you have to recognize what weighs you to avoid it.

How do I notice that I am particularly burdened?

_____

_____

_____

_____

Which stressful situations are already known to me?

_____

_____

_____

_____

Which of these situations can I avoid?

_____
_____
_____
_____

How do I do it?

_____
_____
_____

Which situations or circumstances lead to overloading in the medium term?

_____
_____
_____
_____

What can I do about it?

_____
_____
_____
_____

If I cannot avoid the above situations, I have to be able to do something about the stress that comes with it. So what can I do if I feel the strain inside me?

_____

_____

_____

What can I do after the stressful situation to regain my balance?

_____

_____

_____

_____

What did not help me in such situations?

_____

_____

_____

_____

What helps with strong feelings?

Borderliner's are often overwhelmed by their strong feelings. But feelings can also be influenced by one's own behavior. That is why it is important to recognize the connection between feelings and one's own behavior.

What symptoms of your disease do you want to get a grip on?

(Disturbed eating habits, depression, addictions, self-harm, compulsive behavior, anxiety, etc.)

_____

_____

_____

What have you ever tried to mitigate your symptoms?

_____

_____

_____

What helped, what did not?

_____

_____

_____

_____

What measures do you still know that might be helpful but that you have not tried yet?

_____

_____

_____

_____

Which of these would you like to try?

_____

_____

_____

_____

Many Borderliners are overwhelmed by their feelings. Which are you?

_____

_____

_____

_____

Could you get this feeling under control? If yes how?

_____

_____

_____

_____

Do you know any other strategies you have not tried yet?

_____

_____

_____

_____

Which of these do you want to try?

_____

_____

_____

Borderliner disease often includes self-injurious behavior. However, the environment can protect against it.

What can you do if you notice that you are on your way to self-harm? How can I get rid of the pressure?

(Jogging, calling friends, etc.)

_____

_____

_____

_____

What do I intend to do in the next attack?

_____

_____

_____

_____

_____

_____

_____

AGREEMENTS WITH THE FAMILY, FRIENDS AND DOCTORS

Many people do not know how to behave when confronted with borderline disease. Often they are insecure, forgiving or reacting wrongly. Only you yourself know how you want to and need to be treated when a crisis is approaching. So tell this to the affected people!

Note, however, that the agreements should not further aggravate the crisis.

Who can help me when I'm not feeling well?

_____

_____

_____

_____

How should my family, friends, behave when the following symptoms occur?

Symptom:

_____

_____

_____

Meaningful Behavior

_____

_____

_____

Symptom:

_____

_____

_____

Meaningful Behavior

_____

_____

_____

Symptom:

_____

_____

_____

Meaningful Behavior

_____

_____

_____

_____

_____

Which reactions are not good for you?

_____

_____

_____

_____

What topics should I talk to my doctor about, which has not been discussed yet?

_____

_____

_____

_____

Consultation with the Clinic

If you need to go to a clinic because the crisis is too severe, you should carefully complete the following section. In such a case, you may not be able to raise the necessary issues.

What should be done before you are taken to a clinic? Which people need to be notified, which doctors, who might be able to avoid hospitalization?

_____

_____

_____

_____

Who should take you to a clinic? How should one behave?

_____

_____

_____

_____

What should the treatment look like? Which clinic should it be?

_____

_____

_____

What can positively support my stay in the clinic? Who can visit me? Which therapy? How should the relatives behave?

_____

_____

_____

What is worse for me in such a situation?

_____

_____

_____

_____

_____

_____

THE DIALECTIC BEHAVIORAL THERAPY - DBT AT BORDERLINE

It also turned out that this therapy is particularly well suited for borderline patients. This form of therapy includes a special concept for chronic suicidal patients with borderline.

Dialectic Behavioral Therapy is derived from cognitive behavioral therapy and has been specifically modified by Linehan to borderline. Many studies have proven their efficacy, especially with borderline.

The DBT relies fundamentally on an adaptable, flexible treatment structure, but with fixed goals and strategies.

Adaptable and flexible because, in the daily life of the patient, new difficulties can occur, and must be reacted to, without getting bogged down and endanger the success of treatment.

A determination of the causes of the disease, the problems that arise from the disease, unfavorable factors that aggravate the disease or cause seizures and behaviors that improve the symptoms, takes place in the same scheme as in the cognitive-behavioral learning and change theory.

The fact that the patient can change his behavior requires relatively profound measures. He has to question his views on certain aspects of his life, such as relationships or social relationships with other people, and thereby learn to recognize his wrongdoing so that he can change the misconduct. So he must realize that the typical black-and-white thinking that occurs in borderline disease is part of the disease and that it has an adverse effect on himself and his environment so that he can eventually change it.

For this, it is also necessary to endure criticism, to become aware of one's own feelings and to keep them under control; feelings must also be able to be expressed, without getting angry immediately. It has to be learned in order to behave differently.

The DBT is divided into 5 so-called modules

These modules are:

Attentiveness

Stress tolerance

Conscious handling of emotions

Self-worth

Interpersonal skills

But before we proceed with the description of the individual modules, it should be said that there is no single solution for all patients that brings healing. However, these modules can bring a lot of suggestions that can help those affected. One can, therefore, see these modules as a kind of basic equipment for life with borderline, basic equipment that the Borderliner can fall back on in certain situations.

These modules have to be practiced for a long time, sometimes a lot of trial and error is necessary. But if you are safe in these exercises, a kind of personal "emergency kit" can be put together with exercises that help you very well.

The Inner Mindfulness module

Mindfulness should show the patient who he is. What do I feel, what do I think, and what am I doing? The affected person should stay in the present, not flee into the past, the future or a dream world. He should learn to concentrate on one thing, e.g. his surroundings. He should learn to understand this without evaluating it.

The aim of the exercise is to sharpen the senses for his thoughts, feelings and actions, without evaluating them (not at all negatively), and to manage to reconcile his mind and his actions.

The module "Conscious handling of feelings"

Which feelings do I feel? What does this trigger in me?

The sufferer should learn to perceive his feelings and to recognize or classify them. It also learns which feeling triggers which reaction. The meaning behind it is that feelings can be recognized and controlled, so that, e.g. from a small nothingness, no large tantrum can arise. Also, actions that are triggered by certain emotions should be getting under control.

The module "self-esteem"

The affected person should learn that he too is worth something. The attitude to oneself should be improved; they should learn to pay attention to their self, to love oneself and to care for oneself. The aim of the exercise is to build a healthy self-confidence and self-acceptance.

The module "Stress tolerance"

The patient should learn to endure stress better, to endure difficult situations. The crisis should be dealt with better through these exercises; in addition, a crisis-promoting behavior of the borderline patient should be avoided.

The Module "Interpersonal Skills"

Borderliners also have needs that they often neglect. So you have to learn to enforce your own needs to a reasonable degree without colliding with your fellow human beings. The patient should also learn to recognize and avoid inappropriate behavior. Social competence should be strengthened.

Here you will find some skills that a patient should learn to better cope with his illness. These include tension regulation, the control of emotions and interpersonal skills.

The DBT usually extends over 2 years and is carried out on an outpatient basis. Here, four components are involved: individual therapy sessions, telephone counselling in crisis situations or questions, learning the skills and to monitor the success of therapy.

Mentalization-based psychotherapy

The mentalization-based psychotherapy was developed by the English psychiatrist and psychoanalyst Anthony W. Bateman and an English psychologist and psychoanalyst, Peter Fonagy.

This form of therapy is based on the so-called mentalization model developed by Peter Fonagy and the psychologist and psychoanalyst Mary Target.

The aim of this form of therapy is that the sufferer learns to better understand the thoughts and wishes and the convictions of his fellow human beings as well as his own.

This understanding is called mentalization; that is, the recognition that thoughts are the foundations and triggers of actions. Especially self-knowledge of one's own thoughts that is self-reflection should be increased in this way.

In a "natural" way, a sense of self arises through an affectionate attachment to the primary caregivers, usually the parents. This commitment and interaction with each other is the prerequisite for the development of social contacts as well as the reflection on oneself and the development of a certain sensitivity of others.

The therapy works in a similar way: when the person concerned realizes that other people are dealing with him, he begins to think about what others think and / or appreciate. He, therefore, reflects on himself and his behavior takes on the position of others and thereby recognizes the view and thinking of others.

A "healthy" mentalizing ability enables, inter alia:

The recognition of one's own feelings in difficult situations as well as the naming of them. You can also see what triggered these feelings. To recognize or to imagine what is going on in our fellow human beings, and at the same time to know that one can also be wrong. Knowing that every person can experience the same situation differently.

To be able to deal with and resolve conflicts.

To bring forward one's own ideas and wishes successfully, because one can assess the situation and fellow human beings.

To be able to relate to another person and also to acknowledge his own mistakes and "imperfections".

To endure the fear of abandonment.

To feel valued, to develop your own healthy identity.

Of course, the best way to develop those skills is with a suitable counterpart, with someone you can trust, who you are not ashamed of, or who you do not play.

Mentalization-based psychotherapy was developed for the treatment of borderliners. It is carried out both as a single therapy and as group therapy. In addition, the therapy can be performed inpatient or semi-stationary.

The classic psychoanalysis

Classical psychoanalysis was developed by Sigmund Freud. Sigmund Freud was of the opinion that every person has developed a typical "basic pattern" according to which he behaves and which constitutes his qualities. For example, it determines how conflicts are treated or how relationships with other people take place.

The basic pattern influences our thinking and acting and sits in our subconscious. The basic pattern is unconsciously used again and again for similar situations so that relationships always run in a similar way or conflicts are experienced in a similar way.

In therapy, the patient tells what he thinks and feels; he tells of his fears or dreams. This form of conversation is called free association.

In the course of these conversations, the doctor will recognize basic patterns that he can pick up and try to process or change with the patient.

The classic form of the session looks like the patient is lying on the famous couch, the doctor sitting behind him. So a distraction of the patient should be avoided.

A session usually lasts 45 minutes, ideally two sessions per week. The number of sessions is about 150 to 250, so there is a long way to go for the patient.

This form of psychoanalysis hardly takes place today.

The analytic psychotherapy

Analytical psychotherapy and psychoanalysis have the same origin.

But as psychoanalysis takes a long time, a tighter, faster procedure has been developed: analytic psychotherapy.

A big difference to psychoanalysis is that it assumes that childhood conflicts have not been fully processed and pose problems in adulthood. These conflicts are tried to treat or work up and so to cure the disease.

This is the big difference to psychoanalysis, which assumes that patterns from childhood to adulthood cannot be changed.

Here, too, a session lasts 45 minutes, in the best case two sessions per week; the total number of sessions can go up to 250 sessions. However, this type of therapy is designed so that faster success can be achieved.

The depth psychological psychotherapy

Depth psychological psychotherapy has the same origin as classical psychoanalysis. But there are some big differences.

The depth psychological approach deals with current conflicts. The problems that currently exist are based on childhood experiences. The goal is to change the current situation.

Since different depth-psychological procedures are based on this principle, deep psychology-based psychotherapy is actually an umbrella term for such procedures.

During a therapy session, the doctor and the patient sit opposite each other, so the patient sees the doctor. This results in a normal conversation situation in which the patient can see the reactions of the doctor. This is the so-called countertransference; this is receiving the reactions of the doctor by the patient, which can thus draw conclusions from the doctor's reactions.

This form of therapy can take place in individual sessions or in group sessions. The duration of a session usually takes 45 minutes and takes place once a week. How many sessions take place depends on the success of the therapy. Deep psychology-based psychotherapy is the most frequently performed type of psychotherapy.

The dynamic psychotherapy

Psychologist Annemarie Dührssen developed dynamic psychotherapy in the 1950's. This form of therapy is actually a deep psychology-based procedure but has its roots in psychoanalysis.

The experience of everyday life, together with drastic experiences, can unconsciously lead to erroneous developments. One focus of the therapy is the experience of the environment by the patient, how he masters his life, how he relates to the environment, and how his self-esteem is. Typical appearances are statements such as "I cannot do this", "I can do it alone" or "Nobody loves me". These statements are so deep in the patient that he acts accordingly. Due to these negative attitudes, however, he has a negative effect on his fellow human beings, so that he also receives negative reactions, a vicious circle that must be broken.

During therapy, the patient's self-confidence is rebuilt, so that positive reaction can occur in everyday life. This form of therapy is carried out in individual sessions. There will be up to 60 sessions, which may be held at irregular intervals.

The conversation therapy

Carl Ransom Rogers is considered the "inventor" of psychotherapy. It is a self-contained form of therapy that relies less on certain methods but on the relationship between the doctor and the patient. This relationship should be determined by openness and acceptance by a certain consensus and empathy.

Every person has a certain idea of what he wants to be and what he wants to do. This is called a self-concept. If a person's self-conception is actually calm and balanced, but he gets into a situation where he becomes loud and hectic, it can lead to internal conflicts. He does not feel like himself or incongruent.

Such contradictions should be found in therapy. Fewer incidents from the past aren't the topic, but current events. In an open conversation, such as current events and problems are worked out.

Through the acceptance of the patient by the doctor, the patient learns to accept that such incongruent behavior can be quite normal and gains a greater sense of self-worth. The patient's perception is thus changed so that he can recognize his behavior and problems and change his behavior.

Action-oriented procedures

The basis of the action-oriented procedures is current events, less the subconscious or conflicts of childhood.

To cope with current events, exercises are trained to change the behavior of the person affected. Disruptions should be avoided.

The basis of action-oriented procedures is the learning-theoretical concept of behaviorism.

Behaviorism, i.e. how a person behaves or what he feels, assume that every behavior of a person can be explained by the so-called stimulus-response linkage.

Everything has a cause and an impact.

In behaviorism, this pattern is applied to human behavior. If, for example, rude behavior of a fellow human being triggers a borderline attack, it is to be trained not to let this attack arise.

If one practices such behavior often enough, then the patient is able to apply this also in everyday life successfully. One speaks in this context of behavioral therapy.

The Behavioral Therapy

The goal of behavioral therapy is for the patient to recognize what triggers his symptoms.

The theory assumes that behavior and feelings arise through the recognition of events. If a human being has disturbed behavior, an attempt is made to find out and change this disturbing cognition. An example: if someone is afraid of spiders, then he recognizes something threatening or disgusting in the spider. So it should be learned that the spider is not dangerous (unless it is poisonous) or disgusting.

The root cause of the conflict is not a foregone conclusion. Why it came to the wrong conclusion, does not really matter. Rather, this misjudgment should be "forgotten" and replaced by a healthy one.

One basis for this is the learning of self-control. To stick with the spider in the above example: Without self-control, the patient will never learn to touch a spider and realize that it is not disgusting at all, as it is likely to take off immediately. So he has to face the situation so that he gets the opportunity to recognize his wrongdoing.

Behavioral therapy can be carried out in groups or in individual therapy. Normally, up to 40 sessions are held.

In these therapy sessions, role-playing games, training to solve problems, confrontation with fears (see spider) or even desensitization can be carried out, different ways to change a disturbing behavior or at least make it bearable.

The Therapeutic Search - Or: How do I know if a therapist suits me?

When it comes to psychotherapy, two things are important for it to succeed: the right method and the right therapist.

While the method is selected by the therapist and hopefully suits you, there is the initial problem of finding the right therapist. Because the problem is: the right therapist does not exist! He must fit with you; he must be able to respond to you just as you must trust him. They need to feel secure and taken seriously, so the relationship, the "chemistry", must be right. If you think you cannot talk about everything or if you feel uncomfortable, it's usually the wrong therapist.

That's why "taster lessons" usually take place at the beginning of therapy. Here, the doctor and the patient can get to know each other and assess whether they fit together.

A few things to watch out for:

Already at the first call or the first contact: How does the therapist get over, does he have a pleasant voice, does he seem hectic?

During the sessions: Does he have enough time for you, is he constantly interrupted by the phone or his office help?

Does he answer all your questions in detail, or do you feel rejected?

Is he sufficiently trained for you? Does he already have experience with your clinical picture?

How long should the therapy last, what does he plan to do? Does he poke in the fog or does he know where to go?

Do I feel comfortable with him?

If the therapist suits you, then it is important to choose the right therapy. You cannot proceed according to Scheme 08/15; every patient needs "his" therapy. Let the therapist explain what he plans to do and what the "timetable" looks like. If you do not agree with the procedure during the therapy, say so too! If you are prescribed medication, ask for effects and side effects!

After some time, the first successes should be noticeable. If this does not happen, ask the therapist if this is normal, and if not, what may be wrong. Since therapy usually takes a maximum of 100 hours, but usually shorter, successes should not be too long in coming. Otherwise, the therapy will be over some time, and you are still not healthy.

INNER MINDFULNESS

Inner mindfulness is an essential part of Dialectic Behavioral Therapy.

The inner mindfulness is the way to reconcile our minds and our emotions and to allow an intuitive understanding and knowledge.

In certain situations, it is necessary to approach a situation rationally and intellectually. This is necessary, for example, in case of technical problems or if you have to communicate specific facts about others. But one should not forget that there are also situations that cannot be solved rationally, here the feeling is needed. Everyone has opinions, even if some try to hide them. And straight borderliners have very strong feelings that they sometimes cannot handle. They are overwhelmed by them.

Feelings in themselves can be very positive; you can even see them as a cornerstone of our civilization. Where would we be if no one had a spark of compassion, or no compassion, or the feeling of caring for his family? Where would we be without love? Emotions are, therefore, an important part of humans.

Unfortunately, borderliners have an excess of feelings and feelings that they cannot cope with. So it's important to properly assess and respond to these feelings without being overwhelmed by them. It might be argued that in our so bureaucratic and technical world, more emotion is desirable and that more "gut decisions" would be more beneficial. This is true in some areas, but not for a borderliner. Borderline patients need to learn that they should not always indulge in their feelings, but, if the internal pressure becomes too great, think rationally to avoid self-harm attacks or the like.

Incidentally, negative feelings also increase, for example, due to illnesses, too little sleep, alcohol, hunger, indigestion, malnutrition, stress or specific threats or dangers. Being permanently exposed to such factors can cause anxiety or even depression.

This is where the inner mindfulness comes in, or in this context, the mindfulness of oneself. The DBT should teach to recognize and avoid such factors. The patient learns, for example, how he can live healthier, that drugs are not a solution, but only make things worse, etc. So he learns to take care of himself more. The next step is to reconcile feelings and intellect. For people who were previously vulnerable to their feelings, a difficult task. After all, it does not help if you simply suppress the feelings and replace them with thinking, or in the other direction, guide purely thought-controlled processes through alleged feelings. So, you have to learn to connect the two components, feeling and intellect, with each other. This is also called "Intuitive Understanding and Knowledge".

The DBT provides so-called "how-skills" and "what-skills".

How-skills

How is the situation?

Assessment

The patient learns to perceive without evaluating it. For example, what happens when a glass falls off the table and breaks? The patient learns to concentrate on this one thing without giving it a negative rating. He learns to describe the situation and to react to it reasonably. A non-judgmental attitude does not mean evaluating less extreme positive or negative, but completely renouncing a rating. We remember: Borderliners are prone to praise something up to the heavens, and later to render it completely negative. So it should be learned that nothing is suddenly bad due to small negative occurrences, or that someone who has smiled at you is not suddenly the only good person in the world.

Concentration

In addition, the patient learns to perceive his own actions without being distracted. Many Borderliners have difficulties with this, but this skill is necessary to avoid impulsive behavior because the patient can recognize the triggers in good time and can, therefore, apply appropriate strategies. In addition, the patient learns to distance himself from his own thoughts and worries and focus on one thing.

Effective action

This means that the patient learns to do what is possible and necessary in a given situation. But this is not about right or wrong, which many borderliner shave forgotten. We recall: Many borderline patients who grew up in an invalidating environment were forcibly taught what is "right". An own sense for right and wrong could not train. The patient should thus learn to perform necessary actions or behaviors, regardless of whether he considers something right or wrong. This can also mean, for example, that sometimes compromises have to be made.

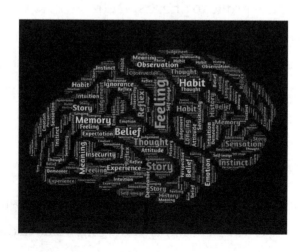

The what-skills

What can I do?

The so-called was-abilities are a supplement to the how-skills. Here it is about observing, describing the process and participating in it.

While borderline patients have so far tried to avoid bad situations or cling to good situations, they should now learn to turn to negative situations and be able to solve beautiful situations too. The background to this is that even unpleasant processes can lead to positive results, or the constant adherence to positive situations can block the patient.

For this, it is necessary to see the event from a certain distance. Of course, this must first be learned and practiced. In addition, it must be learned not to connect situations with thoughts or feelings. So when a situation is frightening, it does not mean it's really dangerous. The patient must learn this in the long term.

And finally, the borderliner must also learn to participate in the situation, which is also called "mindful participation". That is, he has to learn to approach strangers or to get involved with unknowns. He must learn not to block everything that is foreign to him. Participation in unknown situations also means being able to respond flexibly and to possess a certain spontaneity.

The inner mindfulness is the foundation for the other modules of the DBT. It is, therefore learned at the beginning of the DBT.

Radicals accept feelings and events

Often the condition is disturbed (destroyed) by bad news, events or obstacles or rejections. Disappointments and defeats can be difficult to process.

One way to deal with this is to fight back and try to change the situation. However, this is sometimes a self-destructive way because you cannot always change the situation. No one can change a bad grade from now on right away, quarrels in the family do not evaporate immediately and dissolve in joy, and the parking ticket is not cancelled because you do not feel well with it.

That's why the other way - Radical acceptance

Accepts the situation the way it is. You cannot change them now, so why waste your own power?

What sounds a bit strange now actually has to do with the training of stress tolerance, the threshold from which negative influences have a negative effect on your emotional life.

Borderline sufferers have a relatively low-stress threshold anyway, so even slight negative experiences can lead to self-injurious attacks. It is therefore important to raise this threshold again so that pressure from the outside does not lead to pressure from the inside.

However, radical acceptance by no means implies that everyone and everything is good for now, but rather it means recognizing that you can NOT change anything NOW and learn to accept it. So, for example, that the negative notice from the tax office came from the numbers that you have provided, and not that the taxman does not like them. If you are aware of it, you can handle it more easily and, for the next similar situation, learn how to do it better. However, it is important that you do not collapse under this negative situation.

The radical acceptance does not mean, therefore, to submit to its supposedly heavy fate, but rather to learn to accept some things as it is and to fathom ways into new behaviors. Painful experiences remain painful, even for "healthy" people; however, the handling of these pains is learned so that they do not overturn you every time.

DBT's Stress Tolerance module, which includes radical acceptance, teaches how to deal with negative emotions, how to deal with obstacles, disappointments, or rejections so that you remain stable now.

Often you hear, "But my life is so heavy, it always gets me, why always me?", But that will not get you anywhere! It is better to learn how to deal with it and how to avoid some "blows of fate".

Of course, radical acceptance does not come overnight, so a lot of practice is needed. So if a car drives through a puddle again and you get wet, do not try to blame the weather or the driver. The weather is just as it is; the driver probably did not notice anything of the whole incident. And by the way, whining does not help now, because your clothes will not dry faster. Only one thing can help: Take it as it is and try to get dry clothes. If you take a warm bath and / or a good cup of tea, the incident has even come to a nice end. And above all, do not fret.

Summarized again - why should I adopt something radically?

- Before you can change a situation, you have to accept it.

- Even little things can help practice, to keep cool in big trouble.

- I do not always have to be afraid that in the near future a situation overwhelmed me.

- If you do not have a negative situation but accept it, you will never be able to handle it. Alone the acceptance creates the possibility of the solution to the conflict.

Phrases That Can Help

It's like it is

I have experienced lows many times, but there have been nice times too

Even if it hurts now, I can stand it without hurting myself

DRUGS FOR BORDERLINE

When it comes to mental disorders medication, it is about psychotropic drugs. These drugs have an effect on the central nervous system and affect the psyche.

The drug groups of psychotropic drugs include neuroleptics, tranquillizers, antidepressants, but also sleep aids and lithium salts.

Antidepressants on borderline

Antidepressants: medications that opinions share. For some, they are a blessing, for the other devil stuff.

Why and how exactly they work is not yet known. However, it is known that they work! They brighten the mood and reduce the illness. Many patients like to accept the possible risks and side effects in order to get out of their psychological crisis.

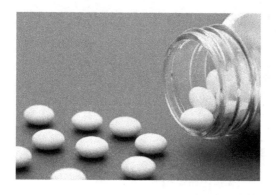

Here are a few frequently asked questions and answers

Should everyone take antidepressants?

> Of course not! You should take antidepressants only if there is no other way of helping. In severe depressive states, however, they are often indicated. However, the intake should always be monitored by a doctor and a therapy to take place in parallel.

How do antidepressants work?

> Antidepressants change the signal transmission of nerve cells in the brain. The messenger's serotonin and norepinephrine enhance the transmission of nerve stimuli in the brain. This is achieved by inhibiting the reuptake of the body's own molecules or enzymes (also called transmitters) messengers. New studies show that these antidepressants also appear to promote the regeneration of neurons in the brain in the long term. In depression, this new formation is usually inhibited and is a cause of depression.

How fast do anti-depressants work?

> It can take up to several weeks for antidepressants to work. However, often after a few days, improvements in mood can be noticed.

Are more modern means better than older ones?

> Even newly developed drugs do not work fundamentally better than previously known. However, many therapists and doctors swear by the newer remedies such as the SSRI or the SNRI and the NARI. In addition, older types of medication often have more severe side effects; newer drugs are better tolerated in this regard.

Who prescribes antidepressants?

> The antidepressants are prescribed not only by the neurologist or the psychiatrist; the family doctor can prescribe such medication.

Which dose should I take?

> Of course, first of all, the one prescribed by the doctor! However, the effect of antidepressants is highly dependent on the patient. Usually, only a flat-rate dose is prescribed, which is then adapted during the course

of therapy. An important clue is the amount of the drug in the blood level, which should be checked regularly. However, if no effect occurs even with a correct blood level, one should think about another drug.

How do I stop taking such medication?

> By no means overnight. As these drugs interfere with the brain, severe disorders of well-being may occur.

This is why antidepressants are slowly "culled out", thus gradually reducing the dose until they are completely eliminated.

Does one become dependent on antidepressants?

> No. An anaesthetic or hallucinogenic effect is not to be expected with antidepressants, so you will not become addicted to them. However, flu-like symptoms or sleep disturbances may occur after weaning. However, this can be greatly reduced by the so-called "tapering".

Do anti-depressants really make one impotent?

> Sexual dysfunctions can already occur with serotonin uptake-inhibiting drugs. If the patient reports on a love life that has been fulfilled so far, and fears that it might be destroyed because of the medication, the doctor

should decide on other medications that suppress this side effect.

What side effects do I have to expect?

> ➢ The range of side effects is unfortunately great. This can range from headaches to digestive problems, from weight gain to sexual dysfunction. However, you can read the side effects as always in the package insert of the drug, or you can, of course, also ask your doctor. And finally, it can be said that side effects CAN, but not MUST.

Make sure that if you are using any other medicines, you can see if any interactions can occur. Some types of medication are incompatible. But here too your doctor or pharmacist will help you.

Description of Various Groups of Active Ingredients

Tricyclic antidepressants (TZA)

This is the oldest drug group. In the fifties, imipramine was the first drug used in depression. The term tricyclic derives from the chemical composition of the agent. The molecules consist of three rings. All TCAs have the effect of inhibiting the reuptake of various messengers, such as norepinephrine. This is why they are also called non-selective monoamine reuptake inhibitors (NSMRI). TCAs have the effect of lightening the patient's mood and relieving anxiety and anxiety.

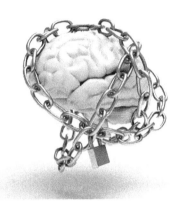

At the beginning of therapy, the patients often become very tired and are very limited in their mental and physical activity. An improvement of the depression occurs only after weeks. Meanwhile, there are newer TCAs that have fewer or other side effects.

Active ingredients:amitriptyline , clomipramine , imipramine , doxepin , lofepramine , trimipramine , nortriptyline , opipramol

Selective serotonin reuptake inhibitors (SSRIs)

Drugs of this category are considered as modern antidepressants. SSRIs are predominantly responsible for inhibiting the reuptake of serotonin in nerve cells but have a weak influence on other messengers. The product has an anxiolytic effect and is similar in effectiveness to TZA in mild and moderate depression. The side effects, such as an increase in body weight, are not so pronounced. Also, an application in people with age-typical problems, such as an enlarged prostate or the Green Star, is possible here. The side effects of SSRI include insomnia and poor appetite but also increased aggressiveness. Since the drug fluoxetine may cause hypoglycaemia in people with diabetes, should be controlled by the doctor for the sugar level of the patient at the beginning of therapy.

Active substances: Citalopram (e.g. Cipramil), Escitaloprm, Paroxetine (e.g.Seroxat), Sertraline (e.g. Zoloft, Gladem), Fluoxetine (e.g. Fluctin).

Serotonin-norepinephrine reuptake inhibitors (SNRI)

These drugs work on the same principle as SSRIs but have the effect of inhibiting both the reuptake of serotonin and norepinephrine.

The effect is mood-enhancing and drive-enhancing. The most important active ingredient is venlafaxine (Trevilor). The side effects are very similar to those of SSRI.

Active ingredients: Duloxetine

Norepinephrine Reuptake Inhibitors (NARI)

These drugs are still very new and inhibit the uptake of the messenger noradrenaline. Side effects are similar to those of SSRI. Norepinephrine reuptake inhibitors additionally increase social activity.

Active Ingredients: Reboxetine (Edronax), Viloxazine (Vivalan).

Alpha-2 antagonists (NASSA)

These drugs block the receptors for norepinephrine on the nerve cells and at the same time and increase the secretion of this messenger substance. They are used in depression, which is characterized by restlessness or sleep disorders. Side effects include fatigue and severe hunger. An advantage of these substances is the strong sedative effect, which can often be very beneficial in the early stages of treatment.

However, a risk with these drugs is the risk that severe disorders of the blood picture may occur. Therefore, a doctor should regularly perform a blood count study on patients and pay particular attention to flu-like symptoms. If the blood picture changes, the treatment may need to be stopped immediately.

Active ingredients: Mirtazapine (Remergil), Mianserin.

MAOIs

These drugs block the activity of an enzyme that can break down a number of monoamine messengers. MAO inhibitors are strongly boosting. However, due to their mechanism of action, these agents may have serious side effects, for example, hypertension. They are mainly used for major depression when other remedies do not help.

Active ingredients: moclobemide (Aurorix), tranylcypromine.

Trazodone

Active ingredient:trazodone

Effect on the psyche as an antidepressant

Possible side effects: Common with Trazodone: fatigue, gastrointestinal discomfort, dizziness, dry mouth, insomnia, headache, low blood pressure, restlessness, arrhythmia. In rare cases of trazodone: blurred vision, constipation, increased blood pressure, confusion, trembling, weight gain, weight loss. Hypersensitivity reaction in trazodone, e.g. rash, in some cases urticaria, angioedema. In isolated cases with trazodone: Serotonin syndrome / malignant neuroleptic syndrome, e.g. sweating, diarrhea, blood pressure fluctuations, tachycardia, agitation, fever, tremor, loss of consciousness. Kollaptischeconditions, epileptic seizures, priapism, liver dysfunction such as transaminase elevation, hyperbilirubinemia, hepatitis,

Drugs containing the active substance trazodone: Thombran, Trittico.

The naming of trademarks is for purely informative purposes. All information is provided without warranty!

Alternative cures for depression

Depression can not only be treated by chemical means, but there are also natural medicine approaches that can help against depression.

For example, in herbal medicine, St. John's wort is one of the best remedies that can be used to treat mild to moderate depression. St. John's wort has a proven antidepressant effect on the mind.

However, other approaches to mild depression are also found in homoeopathy and aromatherapy.

Tranquilizer

Tranquillizers have a soothing, anxiolytic and relaxing effect. Also, they reduce feelings and dampen the consciousness.

Unfortunately, these tranquillizers also have strong addictive potential. After a few weeks, symptoms such as anxiety, disturbed sleep or tension appear. But since these are precisely the areas of application of this type of medication, a vicious circle, an addiction or addiction can arise.

What are the side effects?

Disturbances of consciousness, insomnia, anger, fears, headache, flaccid muscles, impaired movement, mental confusion.

Please note that such medications may affect your participation in traffic!

Lithium salts

Lithium salts cause a variety of biochemical effects in the brain. Lithium is used predominantly in long-term therapy and for the prevention of relapses. These agents can be used in manic and unipolar disorders, but also to prevent relapses or to support other medications.

Lithium is a salt that is found in the human body only in the slightest traces. As with other psychotropic drugs also, the blood level must be checked regularly. Lithium salts prevent or at least diminish manic and depressive phases in up to 80% of cases.

Side effects include, for example, shaky hands and indigestion, especially at the beginning of therapy. Proper metering of lithium salts is difficult because the grade between too little and too much is relatively narrow.

It should be noted in any case that an overdose can lead to poisoning. In addition, it should be kept in mind that the consumption of coffee or other caffeinated beverages can alter the elimination of lithium from the body. So if you change your habits during treatment, you should discuss this with your doctor.

Relatives Of Borderliners

Especially close people, such as the family, suffer from the extreme symptoms of borderline. Relatives and partners can contact counselingcenters for information and contact with therapists. A therapeutic treatment, outpatient or inpatient, is definitely recommended in borderline. In the fewest cases, those affected succeed in getting their lives under control without help.

Family members or partners are involved, if possible, by the therapist. The therapist first clarifies the relatives in detail about the mental disorder. Knowing borderline syndrome is an important first step in understanding the person better. In the next step, topics that cause problems in the family or partnership can be edited. In therapy, the relatives learn how to deal with the symptoms of borderline and thus contribute to the recovery.

Therapeutic treatment can take many years because borderline is a very profound disorder. For those affected, as well as the family, partners or friends, dealing with the mental disorder is a demanding learning process. Support from loved ones is very important to borderline people and favors positive development.

The borderline syndrome is also a burden on the social environment. Relatives must, therefore, also pay attention to their own well-being. Get support and take a break from time to time to recharge your batteries.

Relatives in groups can contribute to the relief. There, relatives can benefit from the knowledge and experience of others. A borderline relationship can also be rewarding if you face the challenges together. Professional support in this way is highly recommended and in many cases, necessary.

Life as a family member of a borderliner can be very stressful.

Many relatives are insecure when the sick person when injured has tantrums. Often also creates a co-dependency, that is, your own needs are neglected, you want to make the sufferers happy at their own expense, wants for him only the best or can be drawn entirely from the Borderliner in the spell.

Whatever one does, whether one reproaches the person concerned or exercises consideration, conflicts are not resolved. Indeed not the behavior of the borderliner changes.

The borderline syndrome affects all areas of life in children. They are often aggressive, are often anxious, depressed and can build wrong contacts. But they are also disturbed on a physical level. Often, they go to bed at night, have eating disorders, are unable to sleep well, have thought or are impaired in their perception. Then there are problems in school.

However, because some features of Borderline Disorder are also healthy behaviors in the development of a child, it is not always easy to notice the event to borderliner. For example, it is normal for children to not always be asleep, sometimes anxious or angry, or even unbalanced or depressed during puberty.

However, it is noticeable in borderline children that behavioral states alternate rapidly one after the other. Just the child was still anxious; suddenly, he/she is overly cheerful. Or children play happily with their friends for a while, and all of a sudden they get angry and beat each other.

Often it is teachers or educators, i.e. non-members of the family, who first notice the tendency to borderline disorder. Especially in school, where a social adjustment is required, these children are particularly noticeable.

In the best case, a dialogue between the teacher and the parents develops so that they can try together to help the child. Contact points for parents are, for example, the youth welfare office or the social welfare office, which can refer to further institutions. Here, parents also find help with education or coping with conflicts in families.

If the suspicion of sexual abuse is in the room, then the child protection federation and naturally also the youth welfare office is a competent contact person.

If the child has a borderline development, psychotherapy is usually the only way to help the child. Such psychotherapy is carried out on an outpatient basis and paid for by the health insurance companies.

There are three types of psychotherapy for children: behaviortherapy oriented therapy, depth psychology oriented therapy and family therapeutic oriented therapy.

The goal of behavior therapy-oriented therapy is to eliminate wrong behaviors and to develop strategies for coping with problems.

A depth psychological therapy aims to find out and eliminate the causes of the disease.

The aim of a family oriented therapy is to uncover the conditions in the family so that a normal interaction within the family is made possible.

In particularly severe cases, inpatient therapy is also possible. If the social conditions or the family environment are not able to support outpatient therapy, this would undoubtedly be the best solution.

The bad feeling of the parents

For parents, of course, it's hard for your child to experience the symptoms of the borderline disease. Of course, parents feel bad when their child is injured or drifted off into an addiction. However, the behavior also causes great insecurity in the family, how this illness could break out in the family, and how one should behave now. Unfortunately, many families try to get the problem under the carpet. The disease is hushed up; it is lived on as if nothing had happened. Unfortunately, this increases the patient's illness because he feels he is not being taken seriously.

Am I guilty that my child got sick?

For many parents, the diagnosis of borderline begins after the diagnosis of borderline. Is it my fault that my child got sick, did I do something wrong in education, did I give too little love to the child, did my partner abuse the child?

Often there are painful months, sometimes even years, before the families.

Therefore, it should be stressed that not every borderline disease is caused by sexual abuse or other abuse! Similarly, not one factor alone, such as the less fortunate education of the child, is a trigger. It must always come together with several factors that this disease breaks out.

It is important for families to get help. Here are questions to clarify, such as how do I behave towards the patient. For this purpose, it makes sense to use therapeutic services.

Rules in the family

In order for something positive to change for the Borderliner in the family, it makes sense to set up so-called family rules, which everyone has to adhere to, including those affected themselves.

Family rules

Recognize that it is a disease

The Borderliner is not bad, evil, crazy, or anything else: he is ill!

He does not kill you on purpose; he does not scribe because he enjoys it.

Find out more

Read on the Internet - for example, with us -, buy books, etc.

It is important to know as much as possible about the disease, to understand the Borderliner!

Stay calm when the Borderliner gets mad

Screaming brings nothing, except that you go to the territory of the Borderliner - and there he is unbeatable. His reactions seem exaggerated to you, but that's the way it is with Borderline. Stay calm instead, show him that you love him. If necessary, you leave the house and come back only when he has calmed down.

Be there for him when he is in trouble. Show him that you love him, that he can count on you.

If you do not help the Borderliner, it only reinforces the feeling that he is alone and not loved. He does not ask you for help because he wants to annoy you but because he needs help! Listen to it, show understanding, show interest - again and again, every time.

When he's bored - Employ him

Yes, you're not the personal clown but: If the Borderliner is in a bad mood and bored, a self-injurious attack could happen.

It does not have to be dealing with something great: bake a cake, go for a walk, ride a bike, go under people, visit someone.

Show Him You Love Him

Borderliners always feel they are not loved therefore, show him that you love him!

Even if he has done something that you cannot understand, show him that you still love him and that you will not abandon him. No way!

Do not put it under pressure

Adding extra pressure to those affected does not help, except to aggravate the situation.

Do not threaten to leave him, to no longer love him or even to ignore him because that's about the worst thing he can imagine.

Do not play the Therapist: Even if you now know what's going on in there and what you can do: Do not play the therapist who can cure it!

But do not be tampered with and wrap around your finger

If the Borderliner realizes he can do what he wants, he will! So show him the limits and do not do everything he wants!

Accept that change is slow.

The borderline disease does not go away overnight; it will take many months. Do not put the affected person under pressure.

Do Family Rituals

Eat together, talk to each other regularly, do something together although sometimes difficult.

Only practice constructive criticism

Make decisions about one another as a parent

So it can be avoided that one is at some point regarded as the good, the other as the evil.

As already indicated, these rules must apply to all, without exception. Everyone has rights, but also duties.

But do not expect that the introduced rules will be adhered to immediately. Usually, it is also difficult for the non-borderliners in the family to get used to the new togetherness.

What else the family can do - show feelings!

Studies have shown that feeling, pointing, and talking about one another can have a beneficial or unfavorable effect on the borderline disease.

Use for this is the term sentimental expression.

There is a so-called high emotional expression, so it is strong and often talked about the feelings. Contrary to this is the low feeling expression, thus the concealment of the feelings against each other.

In families where there is a high level of emotional expression, mental illnesses are far less common than in families with low emotional expression.

So learn to show feelings and communicate them!

For this, it is often necessary to first become aware of one's own feelings. How do I feel? Am I annoying, if so, why? I'm feeling well? Is something scary to me? Why am I afraid?

If you have sorted these feelings, then you should also express them, but reasonably. If you are happy about someone, say so! Are you sad because someone annoyed you, say so! Take your family members in your arms, just like that!

In this way, the individual family members are much closer, but they also take more consideration for each other.

RELATIONSHIPS WITH A BORDERLINER

Even if you have already read a lot of negative things about a relationship with a Borderliner, there is still good news: there are also relationships that can work!

Over the years, relationships stabilize, and behaviors become familiar. The anxiety and excitement of borderline attacks give way to a certain familiarity and serenity. If you realize that the self-harming behavior does not mean the loss of trust or the desire for death, but only from the inner tension of their partner, not so many conflicts arise as at the beginning of the relationship.

If you understand that hurtful remarks or tantrums are not caused by problems in the relationship, but by your partner's illness, many of the difficulties that arise in a relationship with a Borderliner can be removed.

However, it is important to set boundaries for your partner; do not let anything happen to you.

Unfortunately, couples therapies are not very useful; it makes more sense to start therapy for yourself if the pressure becomes too great. Sometimes it makes sense to take a break from the relationship. So you can gain some distance and recharge your batteries.

Here are Some Behavioral Tips in Relationships:

Relationship Advice for Borderliners

Of course, borderline people also want to get involved; they long for someone they belong to. However, if you suffer from a borderline disorder and you love someone, you should still take care to avoid endangering your relationship:

1. Find out about your illness

2. Remember that you are loved in spite of your illness

3. Do not put pressure on your partner

4. Do not put your partner to the test how far you can go

5. If you have fears, tell your partner

6. Ask your partner for help if needed

7. Tell him you are afraid to lose him

8. Admit if you did something wrong

9. Learn to relax to suppress tantrums or self-harm attacks

10. Distract yourself when they explode inside you. Hit and kick your punching bag, go down in the cellar or something. Respond, but not on your partner, or through sex.

11. Do not drink alcohol or take drugs in hot spots. Do not look for sex partners to distract yourself.

12. Learn to understand that your self-harm also hurts your partner.

13. If you find that the pressure in you is getting too big and you want to hurt yourself, tell your partner and ask him to help relieve the pressure.

14. Learn what your illness is from your childhood. Your partner is not to blame.

15. Accept yourself as you are. But not as an excuse, for example, like "I am the same, then I'll keep it up". Learn that you are not bad or evil or inferior.

16. Do not corner your partner. Otherwise, he will probably go forever.

17. Take your partner as he is. If he does something that you may not like, remember that he does not do so to annoy or humiliate you.

Counsel for borderline partners

One thing first: borderliners are always afraid of loss and abandonment, so a relationship with a Borderliner is not easy.

Your partner is looking for the love he never got. Actually, he wants to merge with them if that were possible totally. Of course, that has nothing to do with a "normal" love.

To maintain the relationship, he applies the following behaviors:

- Idealization and devaluation to protect the psyche
- Power and control
- Manipulation
- Lies

In such a relationship, one will always find contradictions. Especially at the point of lies, this will often attract attention, because he will do everything not to endanger the relationship. But remember, sometimes your partner believes his untruths to be true because he has a different view of things.

The relationship between proximity and distance is extreme forBorderliners. Either you are very close or not at all. This is often the case when strangers are not left behind, but you, as a partner, are almost chained up.

Other points that will catch your eye over time:

Your partner really does everything for the relationship

Your partner is afraid to be abandoned

Your partner is afraid to be alone

Your partner is very jealous, does not want to share you. However, this does not happen out of love but out of fear and a lack of self-esteem.

Your partner can not control his impulsivity

Your partner wants to satisfy his urges immediately, even sexual

Your partner sometimes makes massive demands, including inappropriate ones, which you should immediately fulfil

Your partner is constantly seeking proof of your love

So what can you do?

Well, nothing at all!

But maybe a few tips:

If your partner goes crazy, leave him. Stay calm, do not go for it.

Do not criticize your partner; he would interpret this as a loss of love.

You should not run after your partner, because this could give him a sense of power and he would manipulate you.

Create structures for him and set limits to him. If your partner can do what he wants, then he does it too!

Threatening you with suicide? let him threaten. If you panic immediately, he will blackmail you again and again. That may sound very hard now, but it's the only right thing. In general, such suicide announcements are just a cry for love that you should show him. Do not be blackmailed!

If your partner insults you, stay calm; do not go for it because he wants you to be angry. Your partner knows this from his childhood; he can handle it, that's his territory. If necessary, you better go away and wait until he calms down. Afterwards, tell him that you do not like how he behaves, and tell him that you will always go away when it repeats, but you come back because you love him.

Never point out to your partner that his behavior is typical of Borderline disease; he would feel branded and humiliated.

Never expire in similar behaviors like him

Show your partner your love regularly, but not when he asks. He would otherwise gain power over you.

Talk to your partners like a "normal" person, not a child or a teacher.

Do not judge him for his potentially busy past.

Are you there for him when he needs you?

Forget about planning several days in advance. Who knows how your partner will be in a few days?

Do not try to stop or change the self-injurious behavior. You cannot do it anyway.

Do not get involved in discussions about previous partners. You might encourage your partner in his wrong behavior.

If the relationship becomes a burden

Borderline people are constantly on the lookout for the ideal partner.

A Borderliner has frequent and unstable but nevertheless very intense interpersonal relationships.

In these relationships, the sufferer clings to his partner; he seems dependent on him, idealizes him and considers a separation impossible. This goes well until the partner rejects him, then the relationship turns into the opposite.

The more dramatic it becomes when a long-term partnership has been established. A failure of the relationship is tried by all means to be prevented, be it by self-abandonment, by lies, by manipulation or by threat and blackmail, sometimes unfortunately also by force.

When it comes to separation

As there are more and more borderliners, the likelihood of entering into a relationship with a Borderliner increases. But if you cannot or do not want to maintain the relationship because of physical and psychological stress, how should you separate yourself? Because as you might suspect, the separation from a borderliner is a bit different from a non-borderliner.

Should I leave him?

So if the relationship overwhelms you, you should think about it. Of course, we cannot decide this for you; you have to do that yourself.

But even if you want to part with, many still have concerns such as:

That's just the disease, that's going to happen again. After you've been through so much, you may be a bit more hardened by the "quirks" of your partner. Sometimes it was fine; then there were problems, then it was fine again. But be honest: this will always go on.

I Cannot Do It

If you've been tortured for weeks and months, maybe even years, through such a relationship, you're naturally exhausted. So take your time and search for distance to gain strength!

Drugs

If you are already so ready that you use drugs to master your life, leave it! You need your clear mind for a fresh start.

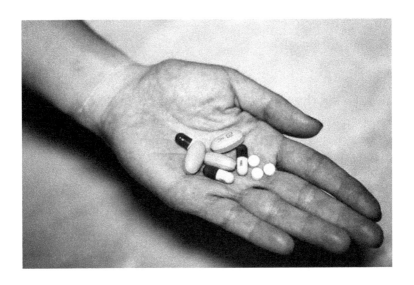

Fear of loneliness

Some are afraid to be alone after the relationship and not be able to enter into a new relationship. So, seek closer contact with friends and family to get over the first time, then after a while, your social life will settle down again. If necessary, seek out therapy.

I have to help him/her

If you just want to stay because you have to "help" your sick partner, that's the wrong approach. But you should be aware that you CAN NOT help at all. Therapy alone can help, and if necessary, it can also be carried out without you as a partner.

The fear of suicide

Are you afraid your partner kills after a breakup? Well, then that's his decision, not your fault. It happens regularly that Borderliner partners threaten suicide if there is a separation in the room. On the one hand, this is usually only an attempt to put the partner under pressure, and one can also call in the police or a psychologist.

The fear that the partner will hurt himself

Well, that is the typical behavior of this disease. He does it in partnership; he will do it afterwards. Of course, your partner can try to take advantage of this and put pressure on you. If he gets hurt, it's his decision, not your fault!

But if you decide to do a breakup, you should also pay attention to a few things:

Do not announce your departure long before

If your partner realizes that he has lost you, their world collapses for them; they may have a strong negative attitude, which can well turn into physical violence!

Look for accommodation

This, of course, secretly. You finally have to know where you are going. A breakup in the old shared flat will not work; your borderline partner will do everything possible to keep you with him.

Contact the therapist of the partner.

Tell him you will part. He can then tune his therapy in time and keep an eye on your partner.

No insults, threats and attacks by your partner. No, we are not in the Wild West now that too may prove to be good for you later.

The moment you break up, love turns to hate. Who knows what makes your partner think of everything? What if he files an assault for assault? What if he denounces you in your area? It is better to be able to prove that he practiced the aggression, not you!

Take everything with you - really everything!

Valuables anyway, but also beloved little things! Your partner will try to keep you on a long leash so that you can never really break the contact, or he might blackmail you with it. Out of his anger, your partner may destroy everything that belongs to you.

Weapons in the household? - Just go away with it!

If you have weapons in the household - and that can be a steak knife - you should make them disappear. As I said, when you split up, your partner may be blind with anger - and who knows what will happen then.

After separation - avoid contact!

Your partner will try to pull you back. He will show himself at his best so that you will see that everything will get better.

So do not give him an address, phone number, even with e-mail addresses you should be careful. And if there is no other way and you have to keep in touch (maybe because of children), you should, if possible, never go to him alone. That makes him the chance to wrap you around his finger.

Borderline separation with children

If you end a relationship with a Borderliner that you have children with, this can lead to additional problems. In general, one can advise seeking professional help. Unfortunately, this is unfortunately not done, which often leads to the welfare of the child being damaged. The problem is that it usually does not work to find mutually agreed rules that take into account the best interests of the child. This is difficult even for "normal" couples, but almost impossible for borderline couples.

In some cases, therefore, it may happen that the common children are used as a "weapon" or as the pressure medium. As I said, this is NOT the norm, but if you are so, here are some tips:

Why is my partner suddenly acting like this?

Well, for a Borderliner, separation can be marked by boundless anger, hatred, and the desire to seek revenge for abandonment. And unfortunately, children are just the right tool to do to the "healthy" partner all that one wants: you can deprive him of the child, you can put the child under pressure until he/she no longer wants to go to the other partner and you can invite the child against the partner.

The well-being of the child, of course, is completely neglected in such behavior, it becomes the tool of the Forsaken, and probably they will themselves be psychologically damaged.

How do I regulate custody?

The normal rule in our country is that both parents together take care of the child. This means that important decisions, such as school affairs, require the consent of both. In addition to being achieved by the common concern that both parents have to take care of the child. In addition, children should spend enough time with those who no longer live in the apartment with the child. Normally, this is achieved by the child being with the other parent on at least two weekends a month and sometimes spending holidays with him or her.

In order for everything to work as it should, it is necessary for both parents to make compromises, and for the sake of the child, they sometimes have to sit around a table and discuss some decisions.

That's what the law says, that's how it usually works, but not necessarily with borderliners!

Above, we have already described that the separation for a Borderliner can cause hate and anger and feelings of revenge. If so, how can the two parents agree on the education of the child? Right: not at all!

It will happen again and again that the child is used as a means of pressure that the wishes of the "healthy" are rejected only because he has left. Alone to avenge himself, just to hurt him. The common custody turns out in such cases than as a dead end, both for the "healthy" as well as for the child.

The child is put under pressure when it wants to the other parent. Moreover, the other parent is always made to look bad, which children will eventually believe.

For the "healthy" parent, custody means that he will always have difficulty seeing his child, that he has to be verbally abused, and that he is likely to lose his child sooner or later. Therefore: Apply for sole custody and the right of residence!

Now many are crying out: The child needs both parents, how can you take the child away from the father/mother, etc. But this is achieved by transferring custody to the "healthy" parent: the child continues to see both parents, can live with both, and can also develop well and develop their own view of both parents. The healthy parent is the only one of the two parents who can take care of it.

If the child is living with the "borderline" parent, it will probably sooner or later no longer be allowed to see / "want" the other parent, it will constantly be in conscience conflicts and will probably take over the postponed attitude of the sick father/mother, That cannot be in the child's sense!

So with the help of a lawyer, apply for sole custody and right of residence. As a side note, it would work well with a friendly agreement, but in such a case, it's pretty much out of the question.

Unfortunately, one has to admit that many of today's courts still tend to think, by default, that children belong to the mother, even though she has a mental disorder or is less suitable for education than her father. Fathers usually have no chance to get sole custody of a child. Unless, of course, they have solid evidence that the mother is not fit to raise the child. For example, such evidence includes alcohol addiction, abuse, prostitution, etc. And even then, getting custody is hard enough.

15 HIGHLY EFFECTIVE MINDFULNESS EXERCISES FOR EVERYDAY LIFE

1. The breath anchor

Your breathing is by far, the essential starting point for mindfulness and relaxation at all.

How so? Because your stress level and state of mind are closely linked to your breathing.

As you learn to be mindful of conscious breathing, you'll get rid of stress, anxiety and worry in seconds.

Manual:

1. Sit or stand with your back upright and relax your shoulders consciously.

2. Close your eyes and place your hand on your stomach.

3. Pay close attention to your breath: inhale deeply through the nose into the abdomen. Feel the breath flow through your nose, effortlessly enter your body, your stomach expands, and the air spreads throughout your body. As

you breathe out, feel the airflow out of your abdomen, the abdominal wall sinks back, and the stream of air through your nose flows outward.

Take 10 conscious breaths this way. Set an alarm clock 1-3 times a day with your mobile phone, which reminds you of the breathing anchor.

2. The Mindfulness Starter Boost

Mindfulness in the morning is probably the easiest and fastest way to start the day directly in a focused and relaxed state.

Most people hear their high-pitched alarm clock first thing in the morning, hang out a bit on the phone, then rush to the bathroom, shovel their breakfast in and hurry off to work/university/ school.

If you start the day hectic, stressed and distracted by your mobile, how is the rest of the day going?

Right. Very similar. Do not do that, and start instead like this.

Manual:

1. After waking up, lie in bed for 2-3 minutes with your eyes open. Look at the ceiling of your room. What does it look like? Do you recognize certain patterns? Stains? Particularities?

2. Sit upright at the edge of your bed and feel your breath next. Do not change your breath. Just watch how the breath runs naturally. Is it fast or slow? Do you breathe through in the stomach or in the chest? Does the air feel cool or warm?

3. Feel into your body. How does it feel? Where does it feel good? Where does it feel tense? Give your body full attention for 1-2 minutes.

4. Observe what thoughts and emotions arise in you in the morning. Just perceive them and look at them without judging them.

5. Bring the inner peace and relaxation generated by mindfulness into the day.

3. Know the body

Often we only perceive our body and are only aware of it when we have pain.

Researchers have proven that mindfulness on the body not only brings relaxation but also accelerates healing processes.

Use this form of mindfulness to energize your body. All you have to do is pay more attention to your body in everyday life. Take 2-3 minutes for this exercise.

Manual:

1. Make sure your spine is upright. It does not matter if you are standing, sitting or lying down.

2. Focus on a body part of your choice for 1-2 minutes. How does it feel? Move this body part in different directions. How does that feel? Which muscles work for the movement of this body part?

3. Put the focus on your entire posture. What is your attitude? Which muscles are tense? Which are relaxed?

4. Particularly effective exercise: "scan" your body mentally from head to toe, going into all body parts. That means: When you start your head on the hairline, go to the forehead, to the eyebrows, to the nose, the cheekbones,

ears lips, to the neck and so on. Until you arrive at your toes.

4. The 3-minute diver

This exercise helps you break out of your daily (thought) chaos and immerse yourself in the only moment that brings serenity and relaxation - the present moment.

Manual:

1. Interrupt your present activity and focus on the present moment and the situation.

2. Activate your senses. What do you see? What do you hear? Do you take certain smells? What are you feeling at this moment? What's your taste in the mouth? In this step, you train and sharpen your senses.

3. Focus on your thoughts for a few moments. What are you thinking right now? Are they positive or negative thoughts? Do not change and rate your thoughts; just observe them and perceive them.

4. Optional: Set an alarm clock to remember the exercise and make the 3-minute diver a few times a day if possible.

5. A bite of mindfulness

Many people loop, stuff and watch TV. Chewing is overrated, who still has the time for that?!

Do we still taste our food in this hurry? Do we still perceive it?

A Buddhist proverb states:

Mindful eating = mindful living

Mindful living = living well

So here's a simple and effective exercise.

Manual:

1. Give your food your full attention. Look closely at the bite on your fork. What shape does the food have, what color, what is the smell? What consistency does it have and how does it change during chewing? What are the taste and the aftertaste?

2. Alternative: Take only the first bite of each meal with maximum attention to you and pay attention to the things in step 1.

3rd addition: drink water mindfully. Feel how the liquid feels in your mouth, how it flows into your body while swallowing and invigorates you from the inside.

6. A digital silence hour

In our time, we are exposed to more sensory stimuli than ever before. Advertising is shouted in from all sides, on the radio, TV, online or outside.

Constantly beeps, rings and lights up something. No matter where you are. This ocean of stimulus signals contributes greatly to stress. The more your senses are flooded with stimuli, the faster you lose your inner peace and focus.

You cannot always escape completely. But there is a simple and effective way to pause your senses.

Manual:

1. Choose a time of the day on which you switch off all your technical equipment for 1 hour. Mobile phone, phone, computer and TV off (yes, even the tablet).

2. Extra tip: Make the digital silence lesson in the first hour after waking up, or in the last hour before bedtime. In these times, you get the most benefit from the exercise. So you wake up in the morning and sleep better in the evening.

3. Alternative: If this is too difficult for you at first (which admittedly was the case with me in the beginning), then

start by switching off the technical devices for 20 minutes and then slowly ascend to the top.

7. Wait without waiting

Love you:

Red traffic lights?

Long queues in front of the cash register at the supermarket?

Waiting times at the doctor or at the restaurant?

Friends, who say they need 5 minutes long and only 30 minutes later to dance?

Nope, me neither! Waiting can be annoying.

And that's why we use these moments from now on to practice mindfulness.

Manual:

1. Feel while waiting for impatience, boredom or nervousness to come up in you.

2. Feel right into this feeling and see what happens.

3. After paying attention to the feeling, focus on your body. How does it feel? Are you tense? If so, then relax the respective body part consciously.

Action tip:

Another way to make waiting for a state of creation and development is positive thinking. With the power of positive thinking, negative thoughts, depression, tension and nervousness can easily be left behind.

8. Feel the gravity while walking

If you look around on the street, you see many people with long faces rushing from A to B hectic.

Do not do that, because you miss a lot of beautiful things and maybe also encounters with people.

What is the genius of this mindfulness exercise? Anyway, we go all the time anyway, and with this exercise, we can practice calmness without the extra time and recharge our batteries.

All you have to do is go in a different way.

Manual:

1. Draw your attention to the activities of walking. Feel how your feet are on the floor. Feel how your heel, then your bale, and finally your toe tips, rise on the ground. Feel how your feet are attracted by gravity every step of the way.

2. How does the soil feel? Is it dry, wet, even, stony, hard, or soft?

3. Now draw your attention to your breath and bring the rhythm of your steps into harmony with your breathing with every step.

4. Variation: count the steps and change your walking technique after 2 minutes.

9. Doing ordinary activities differently

Most of the things we do in everyday life are completely automatic. Mindfulness is about making things automatic, to be more aware of yourself as well.

Manual:

1. Choose an everyday situation and make it different. For example, brushing your teeth.

If you are a right-handed person, brush your teeth with links. This automatically catches your eye because the new approach initially feels strange or unfamiliar.

10. Usingthe perspective of a child

We adults often mean understanding the world and knowing how things are going. But that is usually not the case.

Children look at the world with curious and open eyes. They watch the little things of everyday life with great mindfulness and have a lot of fun.

Incidentally, many of the greatest inventions and discoveries in the world have been made by mindful people who have viewed things from the unbiased view of a child.

Manual:

1. Consider a situation or problem from the point of view of a mindful child. A child who does not judge the situation on the basis of past experience but she just sees exactly how she is at the moment.

2. Realize how this situation or the problem feels from this new perspective.

11. Wu Wei: conscious doing nothing

Most people are constantly busy or distracted in everyday life. They always do something. Most of the time, they act compulsively and cannot even switch off for a little while.

The busier and hectic you are, the more unconscious you become, and the less you perceive of life.

To take a break in this hustle and bustle, use Wu Wei (Conscious Doing Nothing), the effective Chinese practice of Taoism.

Manual:

1. Lie down, sit or stand. Take 5 minutes and deliberately do NOTHING. No distraction. You do not have to pay attention to. Do not do anything.

2. Realize how doing nothingness feels.

12. Consciously slow things down

Amazing: We are constantly developing new technologies that make our lives more efficient to save time so we can do more.

What is this for?

We take this saved time and do a lot more. We work longer. We pack more things and experiences in less time.

This certainly has advantages, but also a huge disadvantage: hectic, hardly any rest, no time to organize thoughts and feelings.

Manual:

1. Choose a time of the day when you consciously slow things down. Start practicing the deliberate slowness for 5 minutes and slowly ascend to the top. Until you find a time that feels right for you.

2. Consciously slow things down and give them all your attention and presence.

13. The 3er combo

This is one of my favorite exercises. No big explanations, let's go to the exercise.

Manual:

1. Pick 3 small activities out of your everyday life and do them carefully. No matter which.

Example 2:

(1) When you leave the house, take 3 deep and conscious breaths

(2) When you close the toilet lid, do it carefully (yes, mindfulness works with everything)

(3) Whenever you stand in front of red light, focus completely on the color of the traffic light.

Note: No matter what 3 things you choose, if possible, feel all of your senses, your breath, and your body as you do these little things carefully.

14. Discover a little world

As a child, you probably did this exercise very often instinctively.

Manual:

1. Find an object, preferably from nature. For example, a leaf, a blade of grass or stone.

2. And now look at this item very carefully. Turn it around, look it over, hold it against the light. Look at him from near and far away. Which structures can you recognize on the surface? Do you see the little patterns on the surface? Which lines, corners, colors and bumps can you discover? How does he feel? Hard, soft, smooth, fibrous?

3. Marvel at the small world of this object for a few minutes.

15. Your finger shows you the way

You can really do this mindfulness exercise anywhere, anytime. All you need is a finger.

Manual:

1. Pick one of your fingers and watch it carefully. What do you recognize? What does the fingernail look like? What about the bone structure and the color of the finger? What is the texture of the skin?

2. Realize your thoughts and feelings. What are you thinking right now? How do you feel?

16. Listen to the silence at night

I do this exercise every night. It relaxes and helps, especially if you have many stressful thoughts in the evening and fall asleep badly.

Earlier, we talked about overstimulation and how it causes stress.

Probably the strongest flooding cause noises. By being exposed to so many noises and noises, we automatically filter out many sounds. We are no longer aware of the small sounds.

Manual:

1. Sit at the window, or lie in bed. No matter.

2. Close your eyes and listen to the silence of the night. Pay attention to what sounds you can perceive. Count the number of different sounds.

3. When it's completely quiet, just listen to that silence. How do you feel about it?

4. Next, look in the darkness of the night. What do you recognize? How does that feel?

CONCLUSIONS

The good mood has become quite rare today. Whether at home, at work, on the bus, in the supermarket, on the Internet, or even in your own mirror: everywhere you meet people in a bad mood - and where the good mood could be so easy. But there are many ways that lead to a good mood - this 9 tips show you the right direction.

A good mood is learnable

Good mood - we know today - can be learned and controlled. In ancient times, however, led mood swings back to the moon phases. If the moon stood unfavorably, one was almost helplessly exposed to his moods.

Even today, one often has the feeling that it is still the case: many external circumstances create a bad mood - whether it is the weather, the colleagues, the mother-in-law, or a particularly stressful situation.

At the same time, there are always people who tend to a sunny mind and let nothing spoil a good mood. Is good humor possibly genetic?

Fortunately, only in part. Another part is brought to us, whether by the parents or the society - and is therefore still influenced in retrospect.

Since a bad mood is a real waste of time, in addition, it can quickly become chronic, beating on the stomach and susceptible to many diseases; it's time for a good mood. Our nine tips will help you:

Tip 1: Nature walks bring a good mood

If the ceiling threatens to fall on your head, you should go outside. Just a short walk in the nearby park improves your mood in no time. It has been proven that stays in nature have a balancing effect and open the eyes to something new.

Numerous studies have already shown that just a few minutes in a natural environment sufficient to achieve a measurable effect on the mind and the body.

Stress hormone levels and blood pressure drop, and self-esteem increases. In the middle of the green, you can relax and unwind. The mind is refreshed, and the ability to concentrate is boosted.

Researchers from the University of Essex in England have investigated which activities work best for the mood of people with unstable moods.

The subjects were divided into three groups:

One group went swimming regularly, the other met in associations with like-minded people, and the third group went for a walk. After 6 weeks, the scientists found that walking in nature had the most positive impact on participants' mood and self-esteem.

Tip 2: Drinking lifts the mood

Yes, drinking ensures a good mood. This does not mean that you need to increase your alcohol intake, but should now pay more attention to your water balance. Because many chronically ill-tempered people simply drink too little.

Everyday life is characterized by a hectic pace, and it is not surprising that many do not take too much liquid. The consequences of so-called dehydration include restlessness, irritability, and low moods.

Since the feeling of thirst is not as spontaneous and unambiguous as the feeling of hunger, it is often not noticed. Sometimes it is even misinterpreted and silenced with a snack or a cigarette.

The ideal liquid for a good mood is water: if you drink at least 1.5 liters daily of it, you can explore your inner balance considerably.

As for the coffee as a supposed good-mood-maker, but caution is required. Researchers from Coventry University in England have found that caffeine improves the mood during exercise, but coffee is not suitable for improving performance.

Other sources of caffeine, such as green tea or guarana, are preferable to coffee, as caffeine is released more slowly in the body. By the way, guarana is also a tasty mixture, e.g., with cereal coffee or with cocoa.

Tip 3: Vitamins for a good mood

Even Hippocrates, the most famous doctor of antiquity, was convinced:

"What we eat determines the mind."

And that's how it is! Many people are in a bad mood, as there is a deficit in vital nutrients.

Vitamin B1 (thiamine) to improve your mood

Researchers from the University of Wales in England examined 120 young women and found that adding 50 mg of thiamine per day over a 2-month period can greatly improve mood.

This is already a therapeutic dose that can hardly be absorbed by diet alone because even the front runners in terms of vitamin B1 deliver only less than 2 mg per 100 g of food (sunflower seeds, Brazil nuts, etc.).

A dietary supplement (vitamin B mix) can easily provide the required vitamin B1 dose.

Vitamin D is in a good mood

The so-called sun vitamin is not only important for the bones but also decides on the good and bad mood of man. Vitamin D is formed under sunlight from the organism independently in the skin.

This is one of the reasons why most people are in a better mood in good weather than on rainy days. It is sufficient if the face, arms, and legs are exposed to the sun for 10 to 15 minutes - but only in summer.

In the cold season, however, the position of the sun is too low, so that there is no vitamin D formation in the skin. Therefore, taking vitamin D3 capsules is recommended to stay in a good mood at all times.

Zinc helps in the production of serotonin

This trace element helps to produce the happiness hormone serotonin and thus greatly influences our mood. The recommended daily allowance for men is 15 mg and 12 mg for women.

Often, these amounts are not achieved, zinc deficiency occurs, and the mood drops. Good zinc sources are z as for oatmeal, Brazil nuts, and lentils.

Selenium expresses itself favorably on the state of mind

Researchers from Swansea University in Wales, UK, have found in their study that selenium has a very favorable effect on the state of mind. One-half of the subjects received 100 µg of selenium daily for a period of 5 weeks; the other half received a placebo. In the selenium group, the mood improved considerably.

The mood-enhancing effect of selenium is due to the antioxidant effect. In addition, selenium protects the nerve tissue and is an important building block for brain messengers (eg, serotonin).In our selenium-poor soils, it is not easy to take daily the selenium dose required for a good mood; thus, although 100 g of porcini provides around 190 µg of selenium.

But who already gets mushrooms every day? It is much easier to use coconut products because the coconut is one of the most selenium-rich foods with 800 μg per 100 g. Incorporate coconut oil, coconut milk, coconut flour, coconut, and coconut water as often as possible into your diet for a good mood.

Saffron, lemon balm, rosemary & Co. are good mood herbs. If you want to spread a good mood, you should definitely use spices when cooking. The good mood herbs includes Savory, borage, parsley, lavender, melissa, rosemary, and saffron.The latter is used as a mood enhancer even in moderate depression and, according to studies, is more effective than antidepressants - but then saffron should be used in higher doses in the form of a dietary supplement containing 30 mg saffron extract daily.

A dietary supplement that can contribute to a laid-back mood. It consists of the two power plants quinoa and amaranth, which are processed in a special way and taken in a special way.

Tip 4: Art promotes a good mood

If you feel that your good mood is leaving you, painting, drawing, or another crafting hobby can be very helpful. So you quickly come to other thoughts, can relax, and the mood turns back to the positives.

In this sense, an American research team has investigated whether artistic creation can improve the mood or not. The study participants first had to look at sad pictures and then draw a picture themselves.It was up to them, whether you tried to trace the previously seen image or whether they drew a completely different picture.

Interestingly, the mood of those study participants improved, giving their feelings free rein while drawing, while those who made only one copy did not set a mood high.So if you focus on the inside while drawing, you can do a lot to throw off your weight and positively influence your mood.

The great thing about this pastime is that a small drawing pad and a pencil are quickly at hand, and the utensils can be used everywhere - whether in the office during lunch break or in the open air.

If the drawing does not give you much pleasure, you can also write down your feelings and let the bad mood out of you. It is also helpful to write down ten things that you are grateful for.Anyone who sees the positive things in life turns his eyes away from what is not going so well.

Tip 5: Special breathing technique for a good mood

The mood can be influenced by the type of breathing. Breathe slowly and relaxed, the mood is better, hectic flat breathing;

however, it promotes fears and bad mood. The following exercise will bring a good mood and can be performed at any time and almost anywhere:

Sit upright and make sure your back is straight.

In the next 4 to 5 minutes, focus solely on your breath.

Let your breath flow in and out.

Breathe a little deeper than you normally would.

Make sure that you do not cramp, but relax.

You can inhale for example, imagine that fresh energy flows into your body and into every cell of your body.As you exhale, you can imagine that anything that annoys and oppresses you is out of your breath.Continue to focus on your breathing and find your own personal rhythm.

If other thoughts arise, bring your perception back to your breath.After just 10 minutes, you will feel more energetic and in a better mood than before the breathing exercise. If you add light a fragrance lamp with special essential oils, then you can improve your mood not only by the breathing itself but also by the effect of mood-enhancing essential oils.

CPSIA information can be obtained
at www.ICGtesting.com
Printed in the USA
BVHW090828030621
608729BV00003B/827